Deportations for Money

*The American Government's Secret
Behind Massive Deportations*

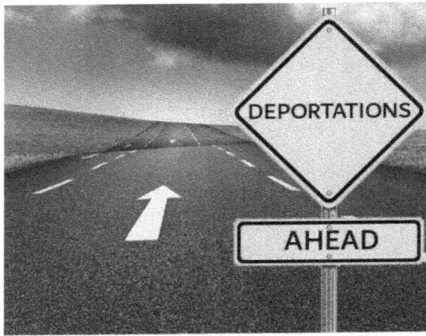

Deportations for Money

*The American Government's Secret
Behind Massive Deportations*

Francisco J. O'Meany

Netequal Technology Solutions
2018

Copyright © 2018 by Francisco J. O'Meany

First Printing: 2018

ISBN 978-0-9998664-0-5

Netequal Technology Solutions
P.O. Box 7122
Stockton, CA 95217-0122

www.DeportationsForMoney.com

Ordering Information:

Special discounts are available on quantity purchases by corporations, associations, educators, and others. For details, contact the publisher at the above listed address.

U.S. trade bookstores and wholesalers: Please contact Netequal Technology Solutions Tel: (925) 478-6150 or email Admin@DeportationsForMoney.com

Dedication

This book is dedicated to my mother Connie, my father Tommy (R.I.P), my wife Alba, my children Jacqueline, Sergio, Tommy, Francisco, Carolina and to my brothers Yuri and wife Haydee, Tommy and wife Noelia, Juan and wife Marina.

To sons and daughters of deported parents.

To fathers and mothers of deported children.

To the entire families that lost all their relatives, friends and assests accumulated after living in the United States for more than 25 years and now live in danger and poverty.

God bless all of you!

Thank you for all your support and patience.

Contents

Acknowledgements

I could not have written this book without the support of my family and my brother Juan's observations as well as his insistence on investigating a lot deeper the United States Government's agenda and cruelty toward immigrants. We are all affected in one way or another by the family separation and deportations performed by the American Government and its imperialist administration.

Thank you for your patience and guidance.

Preface

On November 6, 1986 President Ronald Reagan signed into law the Immigration and Reform Control Act (IRCA) also known as the Simpson-Mazzoli Act which reformed the United States Immigration law (Immigration Reform and Control Act of 1986 (IRCA), 2016). The intention was to legalize about four million illegal immigrants residing in the country, but the INS (Immigration and Naturalization Service) calculated that only half of those immigrants would qualify.

The law required that illegal immigrants must have entered the United States before January 1, 1982 and had been continuously residing in the country. Candidates were required to possess a minimal knowledge about U.S history, government and the English language.

The law also made illegal to hire or recruit illegal immigrants and required employers to verify their employees' immigration status. It also legalized certain seasonal agricultural workers.

After this law passed, millions crossed the border seeking the benefit of this law while others were hoping or speculating that a similar law would be created for the rest of undocumented immigrants.

From 1987 throughout the 1990's millions more undocumented immigrants were "allowed" to enter the country illegally because of the need of cheap labor in multiple industries across the United States of America.

In violation of national and international laws, the United States Government is deporting undocumented immigrants back to Mexico and Central America where they are being murdered. Honduras has the world's highest murder rate, there were 90.4 homicides per 100,000 people in Honduras in 2012 according to a report from the U.N. Office of Drugs and Crime (United Nations Office on Drugs and Crime, 2017).

Undocumented immigrants are being returned to danger in Mexico and Central America in contrast to the heightened rhetoric around the immigration in the United States which is a political battle between Republicans and Democrats.

Across Central America, homicide rates have increased in five out of eight countries, homicides rates in Honduras have more than double and Mexico has seen a 60% increase in crimes, also Jamaica, Trinidad and Tobago and the Dominican Republic crime rates have also surged.

The United States Government wants to deport more than 12 million immigrants and build a wall along the Mexican border, believing that this will stop and cure all the problems around illegal immigration.

On the other hand, legalizing 12 million people cost money, a lot of money. By deporting people, the U.S. Government makes a ton of money, but legalizing them produces a huge liability because these people have been living and working in the United States for more than two decades and have contributed an enormous amount of money to the Social Security Trust Fund, many of them are close to retirement and ready to collect benefits, so the goal is to deport them before they reach the retirement age. A great number of these immigrants have made some life time investments such as homes, businesses, stocks, etc. Individuals living in the United States don't need to have a legal immigration status in order to open a new business, more often these new businesses create new jobs because they are normally established in the service industry such as restaurants, home services, construction, etc.

On November 20, 2014, Secretary of Homeland Security Jeh Charles Johnson issued a new memorandum on "Policies for the Apprehension, Detention and Removal of Undocumented Immigrants" (Policies for the Apprehension, Detention and Removal of Undocumented Immigrants, 2014). This memo narrowed the removal cases that were priorities for DHS to the following:

    a. *Priority 1 threats to national security, border security, and public safety.*
    b. *Priority 2 misdemeanants and new immigration violators.*
    c. *Priority 3 other immigration violators such as the ones that have been issued a final order of removal on or after January 1, 2014.*

The memo adds that aliens should be generally removed unless they qualify for asylum or other form of relief under our laws or, unless, in the judgement of an immigration officer, the alien is not a threat to the integrity of the immigration system or there are factors suggesting the alien should not be an enforcement priority.

On the other hand, people under Temporary Protection Status (TPS) and Deferred Action for Childhood Arrivals (DACA) are facing deportation or being deported because these immigrants have been also living and working for more than two decades and have contributed a huge amount of money to the Social Security Trust Fund, that means is time for deportation.

Francisco J. O'Meany

Introduction

You may be wondering why the U.S. Congress has not passed a comprehensive and bi-partisan immigration law that can benefit all Americans as well as the millions of undocumented individuals living and working in the United States of America.

This book will provide some history, facts, and statistics obtained from several U.S. Government agencies and compiled on an easy to read charts and tables.

It is understandable that most native-born Americans don't know much about immigration laws and what it takes to immigrate and live legally in the United States. This misunderstanding and lack of knowledge is an opportunity for politicians and influential individuals to blame immigrants for any reason that may affect their own interests.

When the economy is going down, immigrants will be blamed; home land security is in danger, immigrants will be blamed; too many hurricanes, immigrants will be blamed; Republicans are losing the elections, immigrants will be blamed, the president has diarrhea, immigrants will be blamed, and for any unimaginable circumstances, immigrants will always be blamed.

Greed and excess run wild with Wall Street corruption, junk bonds and bailouts, and this has nothing to do with immigration at all; domestic terrorists (including the terrorists in Washington D.C.) have nothing to do with immigrants, in fact there are deadlier domestic terror attacks in the United States, such as the Oklahoma bombing executed by Timothy McVeigh, than foreign attacks performed by immigrants, 99% of these attacks are planned and executed by American citizens. Natural disasters happen, and again they have nothing to do with immigrants, and if the president gets sick because he ate an entire box of greasy Kentucky Fried Chicken and French fries plus a cheese burger, now this is your opportunity to blame immigrants for working very hard in junk food restaurants.

Every single time the United States Government gets involved in a political scandal, it always tries to divert the attention of the American public by calling immigrants thieves, rapists and terrorists. However,

1

Deportations for Money

I have seen a lot of financial manipulators (a.k.a. thieves) in Wall Street and a big bunch of rapists and terrorists (a.k.a. politicians) in Washington D.C. and I don't see anyone calling them names.

A great majority of the immigrants being deported are individuals between 50 and 60 years old whom have lived and worked in the United States for more than 25 years. The United States Government has known for decades the whereabouts of these people, but they have waited until now to enforce deportation proceedings.

The economic impact made by these individuals to the United States economy is enormous and it will be greatly affected when their Social Security, Medicare and Federal and State Income Taxes contributions suddenly stop. But the decision to deport these people is pure political and imperialistic rather than economical.

During the Great Depression of the 1930s (between 1929 and 1934), the United States economy was at its lowest. Americans were suffering and blaming the government for the economic chaos, in return the United States Government forcibly deported more than 500,000 Mexican and Mexican-American citizens back to Mexico, one third of the Mexican labor force at that time, claiming that the job competition was the cause of the economic problems and, once they were deported, the economy and job creation will flourish. Nothing of the government's promises came to reality. It was an era of desperation and racism.

It didn't work, no group of American workers benefited from the massive repatriation of one of every three Mexicans, Americans were unable to fill the job vacancies because of their lack of skills, that proved the immigrants were not the cause of the economic mess, to the contrary, hundreds of businesses had to close because they could not find skilled workers to hire, that created an even sharper economy crisis.

Perhaps one day, we Americans, recognize that at one point our ancestors were immigrants and that we should be proud to see how the United States has grown and position itself as the leader of the free world because our immigrant ancestors worked very hard to give us the freedom and the benefits we enjoy today.

Chapter 1: The Land of The Free

Francis Scott Key, a 35-year-old attorney and amateur poet wrote the lyrics of "The Star-Spangled Banner" in September of 1814 and this became the United States national anthem, at that time Scott Key owned black slaves that worked for his plantation in Maryland.

Scott Key's song was instantly popular and he became one of the first celebrities in American life, known from Maine to Mississippi. Key's fame for "The Star-Spangled Banner" helped him build a fascinating career in American law and created political connections to build a lucrative law practice in Washington.

Key became District Attorney in 1833 when Washington had nearly 12,000 black residents, more than half were legally free. An influx of free black people escaping slavery in Virginia had transformed the face of the city and its workforce.

The number of white men in Washington trafficking in people was growing and with the frontier states of the South and West opening up for cotton cultivation enable landowners to contract with brokers to send them enslave and well-built Negroes who could be forced to do the hard work. White families in the Upper South who owned property in people found they could sell them, especially young and healthier slaves for a higher price.

Buying and selling humans was a respectable business in Washington at that time when the slave holding elite had a solid majority in Congress and when President Andrew Jackson was an excellent partner in crime, all under the law.

What Francis Scott Key may have properly written instead of the line "… and the land of the free" was "… and the land we got for free". You may know that people from other countries jokingly call us "United Slaves of America", and I truly believe that because slavery still exists at a different level and with different people but with the same results.

In the last five thousand years, we as a civilization have made greater advances in technology, but our behavior as human beings have not changed at all, we constantly continue destroying ourselves and our environment.

Deportations for Money

We cannot call ourselves the "Great America" when we have a Congress with a bunch of inept politicians in Washington D.C. fighting for their own political gains and economic benefits when the country needs a lot more attention to priorities such as education, job development, health care and immigration.

In Washington, buying and selling humans and politicians continue to be a great business, maybe a lot more profitable than it was back in 1833 but with a more sophisticated system to control everyone and with a lot greedier partners, this is what the United States Government calls "Modern-day slavery".

According to the International Labor Organization (U.N. International Labor Organization, 2016), more than 40 million people were estimated to be victims of modern-day slavery in 2016 and, one in four of those were children.

It's extremely difficult to know exactly how many people are living in modern-day slavery, one of the reasons is that modern-day slavery is a hidden crime that's difficult to identify. Another reason is that there are many organizations providing studies in which they include force marriage as modern-day slavery, and others not. Many, if not all organizations exclude illegal immigration as modern-day slavery, but a lot of countries in the world follow the example of the United States to use people that are leaving their countries for reasons such as poverty, war, prosecution, etc. as cheap labor or sexually exploit them.

Modern-day slavery is sometimes manufactured by rich countries, when the need for cheap labor arises often times, by creating a war conflict or economic sanctions against a determined country. The effect of these actions forces people to emigrate to safer countries. One example of this is the war in Somalia, 100,000 Somalis were accepted to live and work in the United States; thousands are now facing deportation.

Chapter 2: All Men Are *Not* Created Equal

For a very long time I believed that in fact in the United States of America all men were created equal, not until I saw a vast diversity and the huge inequality created by the government.

The Declaration of Independence contains the words that "all men are created equal" and was written by Thomas Jefferson who owned around 200 black slaves at that time and never set any of them free, why? Simply, because he was the owner and didn't care about equality.

The words Jefferson wrote had not reference to black people, because they were considered property, not men and women, and they did not have a place in American society during that time.

For Americans equality is a word that has been interpreted differently since the founding of the country. For Jefferson and our Founding Fathers, the phrase "… all men are created equal" really meant that "all white, free, property-owning males are created equal", women are not.

Equal or equality are words that from the point of view of Americans keep changing their definition, even Jefferson's own definition that "people deserve equal treatment under the law", Americans' notion of legal equality makes no such distinctions. In fact, as Martin Luther King Jr. said that equality is still a dream.

Legal and illegal immigrants in the United States have not been treated equally because the spirit of the Declaration of Independence did not mention them and that is absolutely legal "… under the law".

Thomas Jefferson and George Mason also incorporated the concept of life, liberty and the pursuit of happiness but this does not apply to all men because they were thinking in white, free, etc. Sometimes I wonder if they were real American citizens.

George Mason refused to sign the Constitution based on his principles, he did not believe the Constitution established a wise and just government, but he believed that a bill of rights was mandatory. He also had other concerns, he believed the convention was given the executive branch (the president) too much power. The other two that refused to sign were Elbridge Gerry and Edmond Randolph who was afraid to be associated with something that might fail. For George Mason, he always argued for a three-person executive branch, a one-person presidency was too close to the monarchy they had fought a war to escape.

In our present time the inequality is obvious, men power over women at all levels, rich individuals and corporations getting richer at the expense of poor people, business people taking advantage of illegal immigrants, state prisons abusing prisoners, even a president that can vulgarly insult women, colleagues, staff, military personnel and any individual over a national network television or the Internet. This is how much *our equality* has advanced.

The Roman Empire decadence started with social and income inequalities, that's why our Founding Fathers may have tried to avoid this and that's when Thomas Jefferson made an emphasis on equality, that all men are created equal. But what we now see in the United States Empire is that the 1% of the population controls more than 40% of the wealth, in comparison, before the collapse of the Roman Empire, the top 1% of its population controlled over 16% of its wealth.

The Roman Empire was basically founded on social inequality. In essence, Roman society, at least free people, was fundamentally divided between plebeians and patricians. The ruling upper-class tended to keep all of their wealth and practically forced their slaves to do the work of the typically working middle class. Is evident that the United States Empire in America does the same toward the working immigration class and it is disturbing to see the increase in racism against non-white people. Are we in an unstoppable decadence? You bet!

Insurrections and revolutions are people trying to break from force and power, the problem with these events is that human beings are trying to become better human beings, but unfortunately, they get corrupted in the process.

In the last 250 years, from the American, Russian, Mexican, Cuban, Iranian and Nicaraguan revolutions, we have not seen a change in equality, to the contrary, the gap between the rich and the poor are wider today than it was a quarter of millennium ago. The oppression these governments create against their people demonstrates how low in equality and human rights we have come.

Chapter 3: Two-Way Shot

Most Americans don't know the cost and effort of applying for a United States visitor's visa and how difficult it is to qualify for one, that's because most countries in the world don't require Americans to apply for a visitor's visa when they visit those countries. U.S. Embassies around the world charge between $150 to $200 per applicant and if the visa gets denied, applicants have to wait between 3 to 6 months to pay the fee and re-apply again, this process may take an applicant many years without obtaining the legal visa.

At the end of the fruitless effort, most applicants decide to take a different approach and sneak inside the United States by looking for a smuggler or a person who knows how to get them there, all this for a price. And there they go pursuing the "American Dream".

Once in America, the "American Dream" becomes a nightmare because there is no way to obtain a job with a decent salary to live, pay rent, food, help the family left behind, and maybe save some money for future life events, most likely deportation.

There are no ways illegal immigrants can obtain government benefits because they don't have proper documentation and don't carry the most important "Tracking Tool": A Social Security Number, but the United States Government wants us to believe that they spend a lot of money providing benefits to illegal immigrants, I would like to know how, show me the money!

More than 97% of illegal immigrants do not receive government benefits and they have to work illegally to survive and pay taxes on the way.

Once they have contributed to the system by paying taxes and Social Security for about 10 to 25 years, they get deported without getting anything they have accumulated such as belongings, properties, cars, cash, etc., all that is taken from them (stolen or confiscated by law) without any warning and without the opportunity to recover them in the near future.

U.S. immigrants pay to get in and pay to get out of the United States. What is very interesting is that the government discover (?) they are illegal around 15 to 25 years later, when they have contributed enough so, the U.S. government can declare them illegal, deport them and keep the money they paid to the Social Security Trust Fund, by doing this there is no liability or responsibility from the government to provide benefits when they reach the retirement age! What a business, I begin to like it! It is like having employees with retirement accounts, then fire them 25 years later and keep their retirement account. Ouch!

But, you may be asking "how do they work if they are illegal?" or "how do they pay taxes and contribute to Social Security Trust Fund?", well the answer is very simple: the United States Government provides them with the tools to do so: an ITIN (Individual Taxpayer Identification Number) issued by the Internal Revenue Service (IRS) so they can report their income, pay taxes and contribute to Social Security (Individual Taxpayer Identification Number, 2017). So now, Uncle Sam knows where they are, how many they are and how long they have been living and working in the United States. Clever! isn't it? But there are some restrictions and contradictions from the government that allow them to keep more money because the ITIN: (a) Does not authorize to work in the U.S., (b) Does not provide eligibility for Social Security benefits (but they pay Social Security and Medicare taxes), (c) Does not qualify a dependent for Earned Income Tax Credit purposes. All under the law. Fantastic! isn't it? Remember: All men are *NOT* created equal.

If illegal immigration is a crime, why the IRS provides "fake numbers" to report income taxes? This is exactly one of the main reasons the government is not interested in legalizing or drafting a fair immigration law to help these individuals regularize their immigration status, but since when the United States Government is helping us or helping immigrants? Remember the famous phrase by John F. Kennedy: "ask not what your country can do for you, ask what you can do for your country". My answer would be: "Pay your taxes and don't ask for any returns, fool!". I am getting the point! All these individuals cannot vote but must pay taxes, just because they are undocumented. In 1765 James Otis Jr., a local politician in Boston, Massachusetts, was famous with the phrase: "taxation without representation is tyranny", and believe me he was probably right because the government was doing the same thing they are doing today, no change.

Under federal criminal law is a misdemeanor if an individual enters the United States territory without the approval of an immigration officer (improper entry) and carries up to 6 months in prison and $250 in fines, but if an individual enters the country legally with an approved visa and remains in the country for any reason after the visa expires (unlawful presence) is not a crime, it is a violation of federal immigration law and it is punishable by civil penalties, not criminal and the penalty can be a deportation or removal from the country.

The last report in January 2012 from the Department of Homeland Security (DHS) estimates that 11.4 million individuals are illegal in the United States, this calculation is the reminder or residual after the legally resident foreign-born population known as legal permanent residents (LPRs), naturalized citizens, asylees, refugees, and nonimmigrants is subtracted from the total foreign-born population (Estimates of the Unauthorized Immigrant Population Residing in the United States, 2012). Data to estimate the legally resident population were obtained primarily from the Department of Homeland Security (DHS), whereas the American Community Survey (ACS) of the U.S. Census Bureau was the source for estimates of the total foreign-born population. They should ask the IRS for a more accurate information, well I don't know if this may be legal.

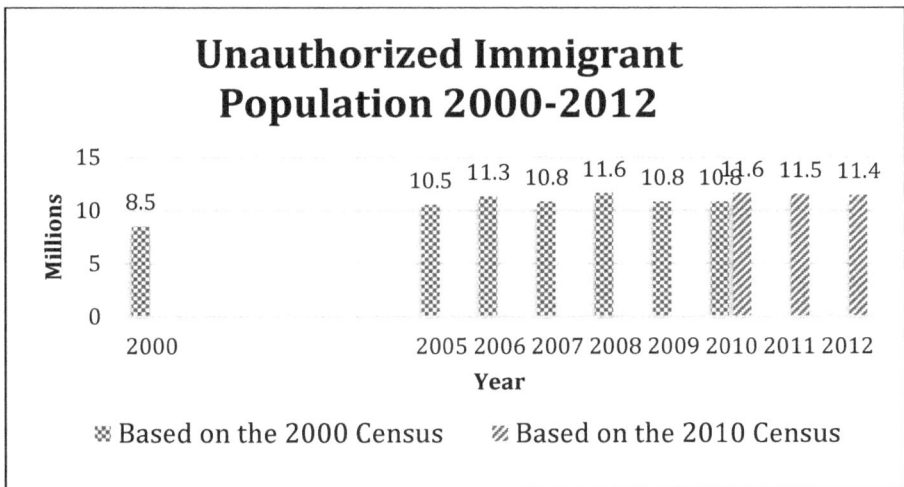

Unauthorized Immigrant Population 2000-2012

Year	Millions
2000	8.5
2005	10.5
2006	11.3
2007	10.8
2008	11.6
2009	10.8
2010	11.6
2011	11.5
2012	11.4

Based on the 2000 Census   Based on the 2010 Census

Figure 1

Deportations for Money

The Department of Homeland Security (DHS) did not produced estimates for 2001 to 2004.

We assume that at least 90% of the illegal population is working for a minimum salary with an hourly rate of $10, 12 hours a day, and 5 days a week. If the money that illegal immigrants make is illegal, so the taxes they paid from that illegal money should be illegal and the United States Government should not be receiving that money so, the question is when that money become legal? This is what the U.S. government and the law call "Money Laundering", I don't know, sometimes I get confused when the law is applicable to criminals but not to the government, maybe it depends on the side you look at it.

We have to understand that U.S. legal and illegal immigration is a business and it has always been, absolutely no one in Washington is seriously interested in presenting a comprehensive immigration reform that will benefit all Americans, unless there are negotiations and money involved or lobbyists from influential corporations that are feeding politicians (look, I said "feeding" not "bribing"), which is a legal action "…under the law".

Chapter 4: Follow the Money

One the most powerful tactics used by the United States Government while investigating fraud, drug trafficking, money laundering, corrupted politicians, White House corruption scandals, etc., is by using the "Follow the money" route so, I am going to do exactly what the government does.

As an example, the following table represents an estimated gross salary for an individual making $10 per hour, 12 hours a day and 5 days a week making $120 a day, $600 a week and $2,400 a month, this is the average salary of an undocumented immigrant and I am being very conservative with this calculation, nobody lives in America with a $10 an hour salary and one job. So, there is one 8-hours full-time job and one 4-hours part-time job to complete the 12-hours a day journey.

Estimated Gross Salary	Social Security & Medicare Taxes by Employee *	Social Security & Medicare Taxes by Employer *	Annual Social Security & Medicare Taxes	Annual Federal and State Taxes **	Total Taxes Paid in 20 Years by Employee and Employer	Total Taxes Paid in 25 Years by Employee and Employer
$2,400.00	$183.60	$183.60	$4,406.40	$5,760.00	$88,128.00	$110,160.00

* Different rates apply for these taxes. The current tax rate for Social Security is 6.2% for the employer and 6.2% for the employee, or 12.4% total. The current rate for Medicare is 1.45% for the employer and 1.45% for the employee, or 2.9% total. Updated by the IRS on April 14, 2017.

** An average of 20%

Table 1

The table above does include the Federal and State Income Taxes as reference because the focus on this book is on the Social Security and Medicare tax contribution (Social Security and Medicare Withholding Rates, 2017).

Individuals working in the United States illegally have been living in the country between 10 and 25 years and they have been the main target for deportation because they represent a major population that have contributed to the Social Security Trust and Medicare funds.

Since the year 2001 the United States Government administrations have deported 6,057,996 (known as removals) and 22,068,993 detained at the Mexico-U.S. border (known as returns) for a total of 28,126,989 undocumented immigrants (source: Department of Homeland Security, press release December 30,2016). 81,603 removals and 144,516 returns have been added for 2017 Fiscal Year.

Immigration officials claim that they are removing individuals with criminal background that are a potential threat to our communities, but the reality is that they are separating families and removing hard working individuals who never have had any problems with the law. They also claim that in order to protect Americans from potential terrorists, illegal immigrants are the number one target. So, the modern "American Heroes" (a.k.a. Immigration officials) are now protecting us from criminals and terrorists which in their books are the illegal immigrants, those from Mexico, Haiti and Central America.

But this has happened before, remember that we haven't changed in the last five thousand years? How about Irish, German and Italian immigrants? Those immigrants were also treated as criminals and also as potential threat to American citizens.

Well, I would like to see those "Heroes" protecting us from the real criminals and terrorists that are based in Washington D.C., because they really have a proven record of illegal activities.

The following tables shows the number of deportations executed by the last three United States Administrations and published by the United States Government:

Clinton Administration

Deportations

Year	Total Apprehen-sions	U.S-Mexico Border Appre-hensions	Remov-als	Returns	Total Deportations
1993	1,327,261	1,212,886	42,542	1,243,410	1,285,952
1994	1,094,719	979,101	45,674	1,029,107	1,074,781
1995	1,394,554	1,271,390	50,924	1,313,764	1,364,688
1996	1,649,986	1,507,020	69,680	1,573,428	1,643,108
1997	1,536,520	1,368,707	114,432	1,440,684	1,555,116
1998	1,679,439	1,516,680	174,813	1,570,127	1,744,940
1999	1,714,035	1,537,000	183,114	1,574,863	1,757,977
2000	1,814,729	1,643,679	188,467	1,675,876	1,864,343
TOTALS	12,211,243	11,036,463	869,646	11,421,259	12,290,905

Clinton Administration Deportations 1

Estimated Amount Contributed by Illegal Immigrants

Year	Removals [1]	Estimated Amount Kept by U.S. Government	5% Estimated Interest Earned Annually	Total Amount Kept by U.S. Government
1993	42,542	$4,452,105,384	$222,605,269	$4,674,710,653
1994	45,674	$4,779,875,448	$238,993,772	$5,018,869,220
1995	50,924	$5,329,298,448	$266,464,922	$5,595,763,370
1996	69,680	$7,292,151,360	$364,607,568	$7,656,758,928
1997	114,432	$11,975,537,664	$598,776,883	$12,574,314,547
1998	174,813	$18,294,530,076	$914,726,504	$19,209,256,580
1999	183,114	$19,163,246,328	$958,162,316	$20,121,408,644
2000	188,467	$19,723,448,484	$986,172,424	$20,709,620,908
TOTALS	869,646	$91,010,193,192	$4,550,509,658	$95,560,702,850

Clinton Administration Collections 1

Source: (Yearbook of Immigration Statistics 2015, 2017) and (DHS Releases End of Year Fiscal Year 2016 Statistics, 2016)

---

[1] These calculations are made considering that 75% of deported immigrants have worked and lived in the United States for 25 or more years, and 25% for 20 or more years.

Bush Administration

Deportations

Year	Total Apprehensions	U.S-Mexico Border Apprehensions	Removals	Returns	Total Deportations
2001	1,387,486	1,235,718	189,026	1,349,371	1,538,397
2002	1,062,270	929,809	165,168	1,012,116	1,177,284
2003	1,046,422	905,065	211,098	945,294	1,156,392
2004	1,264,232	1,160,395	240,665	1,166,576	1,407,241
2005	1,291,065	1,189,031	246,431	1,096,920	1,343,351
2006	1,206,408	1,071,972	280,974	1,043,381	1,324,355
2007	960,673	858,638	319,382	891,390	1,210,772
2008	1,043,759	705,005	359,795	811,263	1,171,058
TOTALS	9,262,315	8,055,633	2,012,539	8,316,311	10,328,850

Bush Administration Deportations 1

Estimated Amount Contributed by Illegal Immigrants

Year	Removals [2]	Estimated Amount Kept by U.S. Government	5% Estimated Interest Earned Annually	Total Amount Kept by U.S. Government
2001	189,026	$19,781,948,952	$989,097,448	$20,771,046,400
2002	165,168	$17,285,161,536	$864,258,077	$18,149,419,613
2003	211,098	$22,091,827,896	$1,104,591,395	$23,196,419,291
2004	240,665	$25,186,073,580	$1,259,303,679	$26,445,377,259
2005	246,431	$25,789,497,012	$1,289,474,851	$27,078,971,863
2006	280,974	$29,404,491,048	$1,470,224,552	$30,874,715,600
2007	319,382	$33,423,965,064	$1,671,198,253	$35,095,163,317
2008	359,795	$37,653,266,340	$1,882,663,317	$39,535,929,657
TOTALS	2,012,539	$210,616,231,428	$10,530,811,572	$221,147,043,000

Bush Administration Collections 1

Source: (Yearbook of Immigration Statistics 2015, 2017) and (DHS Releases End of Year Fiscal Year 2016 Statistics, 2016)

[2] These calculations are made considering that 75% of deported immigrants have worked and lived in the United States for 25 or more years, and 25% for 20 or more years.

Obama Administration

Deportations

Year	Total Apprehensions	U.S-Mexico Border Apprehensions	Removals	Returns	Total Deportations
2009	889,212	540,865	391,341	582,596	973,937
2010	796,587	447,731	381,738	474,195	855,933
2011	678,606	327,577	386,020	322,098	708,118
2012	671,327	356,873	416,324	230,360	646,684
2013	662,483	414,397	434,015	178,691	612,706
2014	679,996	479,371	407,075	163,245	570,320
2015	462,388	331,333	333,341	129,122	462,463
2016	530,250	408,870	344,354	106,600	450,954
TOTALS	5,370,849	3,307,017	3,094,208	2,186,907	5,281,115

Obama Administration Deportations 1

Estimated Amount Contributed by Illegal Immigrants

Year	Removals [3]	Estimated Amount Kept by U.S. Government	5% Estimated Interest Earned Annually	Total Amount Kept by U.S. Government
2009	391,341	$40,954,618,332	$2,047,730,917	$43,002,349,249
2010	381,738	$39,949,645,176	$1,997,482,259	$41,947,127,435
2011	386,020	$40,397,765,040	$2,019,888,252	$42,417,653,292
2012	416,324	$43,569,139,248	$2,178,456,962	$45,747,596,210
2013	434,015	$45,420,537,780	$2,271,026,889	$47,691,564,669
2014	407,075	$42,601,212,900	$2,130,060,645	$44,731,273,545
2015	333,341	$34,884,802,332	$1,744,240,117	$36,629,042,449
2016	344,354	$36,037,334,808	$1,801,866,740	$37,839,201,548
TOTALS	3,094,208	$323,815,055,616	$16,190,752,781	$340,005,808,397

Obama Administration Collections 1

Source: (Yearbook of Immigration Statistics 2015, 2017) and (DHS Releases End of Year Fiscal Year 2016 Statistics, 2016)

Yearbook of Immigration Statistics (DHS, Yearbook of Immigration Statistics 2015, 2015)

---

[3] These calculations are made considering that 75% of deported immigrants have worked and lived in the United States for 25 or more years, and 25% for 20 or more years.

Deportations for Money

Trump Administration

Deportations

Year	Total Apprehen-sions	U.S-Mexico Border Appre-hensions	Remov-als	Returns	Total Deportations
2017	323,591	184,138	81,603	144,516	226,119
TOTALS	323,591	184,138	81,603	144,516	226,119

Estimated Amount Contributed by Illegal Immigrants

Year	Removals [4]	Estimated Amount Kept by U.S. Gov-ernment	5% Estimated Interest Earned Annually	Total Amount Kept by U.S. Gov-ernment
2017 [5]	81,603	$8,539,917,156	$426,995,858	$8,966,913,014
TOTALS	81,603	$8,539,917,156	$426,995,858	$8,966,913,014

Source: (Fiscal Year 2017 ICE Enforcement and Removal Operations Report, 2017)

Estimated Federal & State Income Tax Paid by Illegal Immigrants

Years	Total Removals	Average Gross Income in 20 Years	20% Estimated Federal & State Income Tax Paid
1993-2017	6,057,996	$290,783,808,000	$58,156,761,600

---

[4] These calculations are made considering that 75% of deported immigrants have worked and lived in the United States for 25 or more years, and 25% for 20 or more years.
[5] Based on report issued by ICE on 12/06/2107 with numbers compiled from 1/20/2017 to 09/30/2017, Fiscal Year 2017.

16

The estimated amount kept by the government is calculated based on Table 1 showing the estimated gross salary and annual taxes paid by an undocumented immigrant. These calculations are made considering that 75% of deported immigrants have worked and lived in the United States for 25 or more years and 25% of these deportations are for individuals that have worked and lived for 20 or more years.

Remember that the more time individuals stay working illegally, the more contributions they make to the Social Security Trust Fund. Also, the calculations are made for "Removals" only and not for "Returns".

Immigration officials define "Removals" as individuals being voluntary or involuntary deported, while "Returns" are individuals being returned from the port of entry, an airport or the border.

As an example, the Clinton Administration Collections 1 table shows the year 1993 with a total "Removals" of 42,542, here is the breakdown:

Percent-age	Removals	20 to 25 Years Taxes Paid [6]	5% Esti-mated Interest	Totals
75%	31,906.5	$110,160	$175,741,002	$3,690,561,042
25%	10,635.5	$ 88,128	$46,864,267	$984,149,611
100%	42,542.0	$4,452,105,384	$222,605,269	$4,674,710,653

---

[6] An average of Social Security and Medicare taxes paid during that period.

Deportations for Money

So far, Clinton, Bush, Obama and Trump Administrations have collected an estimated amount of $665,680,467,262 from contributions made by deported illegal immigrants as you can see on the following table:

Administration	Removals	Totals
Clinton	869,646	$95,560,702,852
Bush	2,012,539	$221,147,042,999
Obama	3,094,208	$340,005,808,397
Trump	81,603	$8,966,913,014
T O T A L S	5,976,393	$665,680,467,262

Chapter 5: The Bracero Program

Foreign-born workers have been the great contributors to the U.S. economy, in fact, the United States is an immigrant country where people from all over the world come to work and to make the economy stronger, and this has happened for centuries.

Millions of European immigrants, Irish, British, Germans, Italians, Russians, Asians and others arrived to the United States and their labor helped the country's economic and geographical expansion.

Under the Naturalization Act of 1790, the borders were open and there was no limit on the number of immigrants arriving to the United States, but in 1882 the U.S. Congress passed the Chinese Exclusion Act to prevent the employment of Chinese immigrants.

After the end of the Mexican-American war in 1848, thousands of immigrant workers from Mexico began arriving to the United States easier than European immigrants since they could only cross the southern border and they were able to find jobs in mining, farming, and other industries.

In 1924 the United States created the Border Patrol, which made the access to jobs more difficult to Mexican workers. The World War I created a great immigration from Europe and a greater demand for Mexican workers, but when the Great Depression arrived, Mexican workers were seen as a threat and were used to justify the bad economy, to the point that hundreds of thousands were deported including U.S. Citizens. This is a practice that the United States Government uses to blame on immigrants its bad capitalistic failures.

The World War II created another labor shortage and the United States Government quickly looked down south to bring cheap labor, but this time with a different approach: "An Agricultural Workers Program" which was known as "The Bracero Program".

On July 23, 1942 the Mexican Farm Labor Agreement with Mexico was initiated by an Executive Order and was made effective on August 4, 1942 to contract workers from Mexico. The final version of the agreement was released on April 26, 1943 and was signed by representatives from both countries. From Mexico, Ernesto Hidalgo, representative of Foreign Affairs Ministry and Abraham J. Navas, representative of the Ministry of Labor. From the United States, Joseph

Deportations for Money

F. McGurk, Counsel of the American Embassy in Mexico, John O. Walker, Assistant Administrator of Farm Security Administration, United States Department of Agriculture, and David O. Meeker, Assistant, Office of Agricultural War Relations. The agreement was extended with the Migrant Labor Agreement of 1951 and was enacted as an amendment to the Agricultural Act of 1949, known as Public Law 78, by the U.S. Congress which set the official parameters for the program until its termination in 1964.

The Mexican workers were called "*Braceros*" because they worked with their arms and hands (bracero comes from the Spanish word *Brazo* or arm). During the same period, and taking advantage of cheap labor, railroad companies negotiated an independent contract to import Mexicans to the United States, primarily as maintenance workers. The *braceros* helped to sustain agricultural production during the war and were an important work force in maintaining railroad lines for the transportation of goods, war materials, and people.

Nearly 5 million Mexicans made the journey to the United States and entered under a six-month or twelve-month contract and were assigned to regions throughout the country. Once the contract expired, each *bracero* was required to return to Mexico and sign another contract in order to return to the United States to work.

General provisions of the agreement were:

- Mexicans contracting to work in the United States shall not be engaged in any military service.

- Mexicans entering the United States as a result of this understanding shall not suffer discriminatory acts of any kind in accordance with the Executive Order No. 8802 issued at the White House on June 25, 1941.

- Mexicans entering the United States as a result of this understanding shall enjoy the guarantees of transportation, living expenses and repatriation established in Article 29 of the Mexican Labor Law.

- Mexicans entering the United States as a result of this understanding shall not be employed to displace other workers, or for the purpose of reducing rates of pay previously established.

To implement the general principles mentioned above, specific clauses were established. These included:

Contracts:
   a. Contracts will be made between the employer and the worker under the supervision of the Mexican Government. (Contracts must be written in Spanish).

   b. The employer (Farm Security Administration) shall enter into a contract with the sub-employer, with a view to proper observance of the principles embodied in this understanding.

Admission:
   a. The Mexican health authorities will, at the place where the worker comes, see that he meets the necessary physical conditions.

Transportation:
   a. All transportation and living expenses from the place of origin to destination, and return, as well as expenses incurred in the fulfillment of any requirements of the migratory nature shall be met by the employer.
   b. Personal belongings of the workers up to a maximum of 35 kilos per person shall be transported at the expense of the employer.
   c. In accord with the intent of Article 29 of the Mexican Federal Labor Law, it is expected that the employer will collect all or part of the cost accruing under (a) and (b) of transportation from the sub-employer.

Deportations for Money

Wages and Employment:

a. (1) Wages to be paid to the worker shall be the same as those paid for similar work to other agricultural laborers in the respective regions of destination; but in no case, shall this wage be less than 30 cents per hour (U.S. currency); piece rates shall be so set as to enable the worker of average ability to earn the prevailing wage.

(2) On the basis of prior authorization from the Mexican Government salaries lower than those established in the previous clause may be paid those emigrants admitted into the United States as members of the family of the worker under contract and who, when they are in the field, are able also to become agricultural laborers who, by their condition of age or sex, cannot carry out the average amount of ordinary work.

b. The worker shall be exclusively employed as an agricultural laborer for which he has been engaged; any change from such type of employment shall be made with the express approval of the worker and with the authority of the Mexican Government.

c. There shall be considered illegal any collection by reason of commission or for any other concept demanded of the workers.

d. Work for minors under 14 years shall be strictly prohibited, and they shall have the same schooling opportunities as those enjoyed by children of other agricultural laborers.

e. Workers domiciled in the migratory labor camps or at any other place of employment under this understanding shall be free to obtain articles for their personal consumption, or that of their families, wherever it is most convenient for them.

f.   Housing conditions, sanitary, and medical services enjoyed by workers admitted under this understanding shall be identical to those enjoyed by the other agricultural workers in the same localities.

g.   Workers admitted under this understanding shall enjoy as regards occupational diseases and accidents the same guarantees enjoyed by other agricultural workers under United States legislation.

h.   Groups of workers admitted under this understanding shall elect their own representatives to deal with the employer, but it is understood that all such representatives shall be working members of the group.   The Mexican consuls in their respective jurisdiction shall make every effort to extend all possible protection to all these workers on any questions affecting them.

i.   For such time as they are unemployed under a period equal to 75 percent of the period (exclusive of Sundays) for which the workers have been contracted they shall receive a subsistence allowance at the rate of $3.00 per day.

j.   For the remaining 25 percent of the period for which the workers have been contracted during which the workers may be unemployed they shall receive subsistence on the same bases that are established for farm laborers in the United States.

k.   Should the cost of living rise this will be a matter for reconsideration.

l.   The master contracts for workers submitted to the Mexican Government shall contain definite provisions for computation of subsistence and payments under this understanding.

Deportations for Money

Saving Fund
a. The respective agency of the Government of the United States shall be responsible for the safekeeping of the sums contributed by the Mexican workers towards the formation of their Rural Savings Fund, until such sums are transferred to the Mexican Agricultural Credit Bank, which shall assume responsibilities for the deposit, for their safekeeping and for the application, or, in the absence of these, for their return.

This agreement was published on a history of the emergency farm labor supply program 1943-47 by Wayne D. Rasmussen (Rasmussen, 1951).

As the old proverb says: *"The road to hell is paved with good intentions"*, the majority of these clauses were not met or even supervised by the United States and Mexican governments, clearly, they were more concerned about the economic outcome this "agreement" was going to generate.

The saving fund mysteriously disappeared within the Mexican and United States Governments. Nobody knows exactly how much money was deducted from these workers.

Those hard-working individuals came to the United States in times when we needed their work, they followed the rules imposed on the contracts and did all that was asked of them, in return they were abused and exploited.

The majority of these *braceros* have already died, but in January 2001 a group of surviving former braceros showed up at the federal courthouses in San Francisco California and Washington D.C. to file a lawsuit against both governments demanding that their funds be returned. Both governments tried to get the lawsuit thrown out.

The United States argued that the lawsuit belonged in Mexican courts. After declaring that it was immune from suits filed in foreign courts, the Mexican government argued that there was not documentation supporting the *braceros'* claim. How about the "Saving Fund" stated on the general agreement? Both governments setup bank accounts for the transfer of those funds. The "Saving Fund" looks like a kickback given to the Mexican government in return of cheap labor.

In 2005 the Mexican government agreed to pay out a settlement of 38,000 Mexican pesos (around US$3,000 at current exchange) to anyone who could prove with documentation that he or she had worked in the bracero program. They never mentioned the interest earned on the last six decades. The agreement stated that the amount had to be paid over a three-year period or about US$86 a month.

Experts claim that the Mexican government owes the *braceros* between US$500 million and 1-billion dollars if we calculate the interests.

Generation after generation, the Mexican government has cheated on their fellow citizens, the *braceros* were not the exception.

Chapter 6: TPS, DACA, DAPA

Remember I mentioned that United States Immigration is a business? Well there are some other side business called "programs" and created by the United States Government to provide temporary protected status (USCIS, Temporary Protected Status, 2017) to individuals in the United States and is known as TPS. This program was designed to give "protection" to individuals due to temporary conditions in their countries such as civil wars or a war sponsored by the United States, natural disasters such as hurricanes, earthquakes or epidemics.

Whenever there is a natural disaster or a human disgrace in the world, there is an opportunity for the United States government to bring immigrants from those regions into the country and place them in a "protection status" so they can work and contribute to the tax and social security system. There are more than 300,000 TPS beneficiaries that are facing deportation because the United States Government says that it is now safe to return their country of origin, but in fact it is because they have reached one of the "magic numbers": 20 years or more living and working in the United States, now they qualify for another program "Deportation Proceedings" or "Removal Proceedings" as the U.S. Government like to call it.

The United States is a system addicted to cheap labor and its Justice department is always ready and willing to create laws that can achieve this because there are entire industries that depend on the labor exploitation. The laws are written almost identical as the one created for the "braceros" but with changes to accommodate the new arrivals.

The Deferred Action for Childhood Arrivals (DHS, Deferred Action for Childhood Arrivals (DACA), 2017) also known as the "Dreamers" program was an immigration policy created by the Obama Administration in June 2012 and it allows minors who entered the country illegally and have been continuously living in the United States since June 15, 2007. The Deferred Action for Parents of Americans and Lawful Permanent Residents (DAPA) is a program the provides a path for illegal aliens with a United States citizen or a Lawful Permanent Resident child to be considered for deferred action. There are more than 800,000 individuals living and working in the United States under this program since 2007 and they have reached one of the "magic numbers": 10 years or more producing income and Social Security taxes and are being considered a liability for the United States Government and now they qualify for the "Deportation Proceedings" program. The following table shows the estimated Social Security and Medicare taxes paid by individuals enrolled on these programs:

Program	Subject to Removals	20 & 10 Years Taxes Paid [7]	Total Kept By Government
TPS	300,000	$88,128	$26,438,400,000
DACA	800,000	$44,064	$35,251,200,000
Totals	1,100,000		$61,689,600,000

While those numbers may look big, there are only a small amount generated by those two programs in comparison with the amount generated by massive deportations performed by previous United States Administrations.

Normally, temporary programs are created to protect individuals from deportations but they must play by the rules that are usually a year or two-year re-application process to refresh the United States Government data base of home and workplace addresses, telephone numbers and latest changes on an individual's life.

Once a temporary program ends or the United States Government notice that a "magic number" has been reached, the "protection status" is converted to a "non-protection status" and an individual immediately becomes a criminal and is subject to the "Deportation Proceedings" program and, the party is over.

---

[7] An average of Social Security and Medicare taxes paid during that period.

Chapter 7: Soup of "Temporary Programs"

There are about 185 different types of U.S. visas which are divided in two main categories: Non-immigrant visa for temporary visits such as tourism, work, business or visiting friends and family – and Immigrant visa for people planning to stay permanently in the United States.

The following table shows the current list of (State, 2017) "Temporary Worker Visa Categories":

Visa Category	Description
H-1B: Person in Specialty Occupation	To work in a specialty occupation. Requires a higher education degree or its equivalent. Includes fashion models of distinguished merit and ability and government-to-government research and development, or co-production projects administered by the Department of Defense.
H-1B1: Free Trade Agreement (FTA) Professional – Chile, Singapore	To work in a specialty occupation. Requires a post-secondary degree involving at least four years of study in the field of specialization. (Note: This is not a petition-based visa. For application procedures, please refer to the website for the U.S. Embassy in Chile or the U.S. Embassy in Singapore.
H-2A: Temporary Agricultural Worker	This program allows U.S. employers or U.S. agents who meet specific regulatory requirements bring foreign nationals to the United States to fill temporary agricultural jobs. A U.S. employer or agent must file form I-129, Petition for Nonimmigrant Worker, on a prospective worker's behalf.
H-2B: Temporary Non-agricultural Worker	For temporary or seasonal non-agricultural work. Limited to citizens or nationals of designated countries, with limited exceptions, if determined to be in the United States interest.

Francisco J. O'Meany

Visa Category	Description
H-3: Trainee or Special Education visitor	To receive training, other than graduate medical or academic, that is not available in the trainee's home country or practical training programs in the education of children with mental, physical, or emotional disabilities.
L: Intracompany Transferee	To work at a branch, parent, affiliate, or subsidiary of the current employer in a managerial or executive capacity, or in a position requiring specialized knowledge. Individual must have been employed by the same employer abroad continuously for 1 year within the three preceding years.
O: Individual with Extraordinary Ability or Achievement	For persons with extraordinary ability or achievement in the sciences, arts, education, business, athletics, or extraordinary recognized achievements in the motion picture and television fields, demonstrated by sustained national or international acclaim, to work in their field of expertise. Includes persons providing essential services in support of the above individual.
P-1: Individual or Team Athlete, or Member of an Entertainment Group	To perform at a specific athletic competition as an athlete or as a member of an entertainment group. Requires an internationally recognized level of sustained performance. Includes persons providing essential services in support of the above individual.
P-2: Artist or Entertainer (Individual or Group)	For performance under a reciprocal exchange program between an organization in the United States and an organization in another country. Includes persons providing essential services in support of the above individual.

29

Visa Category	Description
P-3: Artist or Entertainer (Individual or Group)	To perform, teach or coach under a program that is culturally unique or a traditional ethnic, folk, cultural, musical, theatrical, or artistic performance or presentation. Includes persons providing essential services in support of the above individual.
Q-1: Participant in an International Cultural Exchange Program	For practical training and employment and for sharing of the history, culture, and traditions of you home country through participation in an international cultural exchange program.

All the above visas are temporary and workers must leave the country when the specified visa expires (USCIS, Temporary (Nonimmigrant) Workers, 2011). The following table shows the numbers for contributions made by these programs:

Visa Category	Annual Limit	Max Stay	Average
H-1B	65,000	6 Years	65,000
H-2A	No Limit *	3 Years	55,000
H-2B	66,000	3 Years	66,000
TOTALS			186,000

* In Fiscal Year 2011 55,384 visas were issued.

As an example, the following table represents an estimated gross salary for an individual making $20 per hour, 8 hours a day and 5 days a week making $160 a day, $800 a week and $3,200 a month, this is the average salary of an temporary non-immigrant worker:

Estimated Gross Salary	Social Security & Medicare Taxes by Employee *	Social Security & Medicare Taxes by Employer *	Total Annual Taxes	Total Taxes Paid in 3 Year by Employee and Employer	Total Taxes Paid in 6 Year by Employee and Employer
$3,200.00	$244.80	$244.80	$5,875.20	$17,625.60	$35,251.20

* Different rates apply for these taxes. The current tax rate for Social Security is 6.2% for the employer and 6.2% for the employee, or 12.4% total. The current

> rate for Medicare is 1.45% for the employer and 1.45% for the employee, or 2.9% total. Updated by the IRS on April 14, 2017.

Temporary workers have either a higher education or some special skills that makes their salary a little higher.

The following table shows the average numbers generated by temporary workers in the last 10 years and are considered just an estimated amount:

Visa Category	Average Visas	Annual Benefits Paid	10-Year Average
H-1B	65,000	$5,875.20	$3,818,880,000
H-2A	55,000	$5,875.20	$3,231,360,000
H-2B	66,000	$5,875.20	$3,877,632,000
TOTALS			$10,927,872,000

On December 2nd 2017, the United States announced that it will no longer be participating in the global compact on migration, saying it undermines the nation's sovereignty. The United States has been a part of the New York Declaration for Refugees and Migrants since it was formed in 2016. The declaration aims to ensure the rights of migrants, help them resettle and provide them with access to education and jobs.

Secretary of State Rex Tillerson said "While we will continue to engage on number of fronts at the United Nations, in this case, we simply cannot in good faith support a process that could undermine the sovereign right of the United states to enforce our immigration laws and secure our borders. The United States supports international cooperation on migration issues, but it is the primary responsibility of sovereign states to help ensure that migration is safe, orderly, and legal.". I don't think he believes what he said, he may not understand the subject at all!

The United States ambassador to the United Nations, Nikki Haley said "Our decisions on immigration policies must always be made by Americans and Americans alone. We will decide how best to control our borders and *who* will be allowed to enter our country,"

Deportations for Money

Of course! Being part of this supervised group by the United Nations jeopardizes the internal agenda of the United States Government about immigration laws and how immigrants are treated in the United States and how much money the United States Government is making out of the exploited illegal immigrants.

In fact, what the United States Government wants to do in order to "fix" the so-called immigration law is to create "temporary programs" for immigrants to come to work for 3 to 5 years and then return these people back to their home countries and re-apply for re-entry into the United States. The program will give immigrants a permit to work only, they cannot apply for a permanent status or change the "temporary" status that was granted to them, if they do try to change their status, they will be subject for deportation, because they will be violating the law, the law imposed by the government.

If you follow the logic, the United States Government wants to bring immigrants to work, exploit them, make them pay taxes, contribute to the Social Security Trust Fund and Medicare, and then let them return to their countries 5 years later, wipe out all contributions so they have no right to claim benefits, then re-apply for a "temporary job" to return to the United States and, if they are lucky, start all over again! That's what they call justice and equality in the greatest country in the world.

So, the "new law" will prevent us from having 12.5 million illegal immigrants in the country but 12.5 million "temporary workers" that can be used, exploited, abused and then recycled every 5 years, and you know that after 4 cycles (20 years) of doing this, immigrants will not be able to qualify for the job because they may be too old for those jobs, which may be in construction, agricultural, industrial, etc. that may require strength and ability to move quickly.

These "temporary workers" will not have any opportunity to live in the United States with their families and see their children get a better education

It is sad to see that all this looks more like modern-day slavery than anything else, so we are back to the 1700's and the United States of America now looks like the "United Slaves of America" and more closely to the Roman Empire.

Chapter 8: 12.5 Million Deportations or Legalizations

There are 3 "magic numbers" for the U.S. Government when it considers to deport someone that has been living illegally in the country: 10, 20 and 25, these are the number of years that an illegal person has been living and working in the United States, if you have hit one of those numbers you are in the "black list" and probably qualify for the "Deportation Proceedings" program.

If you have lived and worked illegally in the United States for 10 years you have contributed approximately $44,064, for 20 years $88,128 and for 25 years $110,160 in Social Security and Medicare tax benefits, so you represent a liability for the U.S. Government and you are a "subject for deportation", once you get deported the liability disappears and your contribution increases the Social Security Trust Fund.

As of 2017, the Federation for American Immigration Reform (FAIR, 2017) estimates the number of illegal immigrants in the United States to be approximately 12.5 million.

The U.S. Government is planning to deport all 12.5 million individuals that are living and working in the United States since 1992 because they have reached the 10, 20 and 25 years mark or a "magic number". So far, we haven't seen immigration raids because is likely that they are using the "hand-picked" tactic, which is nothing but deporting individuals that have passed the mark of 10 years living illegally in the country and have been paying taxes using the temporary number ITIN (Individual Taxpayer Identification Number, 2017) provided by the IRS. Immigration officials obtain home and workplace addresses of these individuals which make them an easy target.

In 2017, Immigration and Custom Enforcement agents are deporting an average of 500 individuals daily. The United States Government has announced that it would increase the number of agents and immigration judges to accelerate the deportation process.

If the U.S. Congress approves a larger budget to address the illegal immigration and to reach the goal of deporting 1,000 illegal aliens daily, it will take almost 35 years to complete the task and there will be no more illegal immigrants in the country by the year 2052, assuming that there will be no more illegals crossing the border or staying in the country after their visas expired, the problem is that by that time more than 6 million individuals would have qualified for Social Security benefits which they have legally contributed to and are entitled to benefits, that's when the shit will hit the fan.

However, if the U.S. Congress rejects the idea of increasing the budget to accelerate the deportation process, it will take 70 years to complete the task and there will be no more illegal immigrants by the year 2087 and we may be celebrating the new millennium as the first country without illegal aliens in the 22nd century.

Immigration officials are arresting more people who never committed any crime, clogging the backlogged immigration courts. Every year a great number of individuals are ordered deported in absentia, meaning they did not attend their hearings and could not be deported immediately, but more often government officials have their home or work addresses and know how locate them.

You may think that deporting so many people may contradict the main principle of letting illegal aliens live and work in the country because illegal immigration in the United States is a profitable business and we really need illegal immigration to have cheap labor and give the chance to employers to exploit illegal immigrants, the *modus operandi* should continue as usual because this is the modern-day slavery executed with sophistication.

The following table shows the amount of collected Social Security and Medicare taxes that are produced daily and monthly by deporting 500 and 1,000 individuals each day:

Daily Removals	20 Years Taxes Paid [8]	Total Daily	Total Monthly
500	$88,128	$44,064,000	$1,321,920,000
1000	$88,128	$88,128,000	$2,643,840,000

The U.S. deportation priority continues to be targeting individuals that have reached the "magic number" of 10, 20 and 25 years of being illegal in the United States.

[8] An average of Social Security and Medicare taxes paid during that period.

Chapter 9: Social Security Runs Out of Money

It's been a long time since I heard that the United States Social Security Trust Fund was running out of money and that it won't have funds to pay benefits after the year 2020, then it was changed to the year 2040, then it was again changed to year 2035, then I realized I was being stupid by listening to a bunch of politicians trying to draw attention from the American public, now this can change depending on who is in power or who's running for United States Presidency and how much they want to lie to the public.

In reality, the U.S. Social Security Trust Fund has $2.8 trillion in assets at the end of 2016 (SSA, 2016), which much of it has been borrowed by the United States Government.

Social Security is a Cash-In/Cash-Out program that went into the red in the year 2010 when payroll tax revenue came up about $37 billion short of the benefits paid to retirees.

President Obama's budget director, Jacob Lew, told reporters in an interview in 2011: "Social Security benefits are self-financing. They are paid for with payroll taxes collected from workers and their employers throughout their careers. These taxes are placed in a trust fund dedicated to paying benefits owed to current and future beneficiaries. Even though Social Security began collecting less in taxes than it paid in benefits in 2010, the trust will continue to accrue interest and grow until 2025, and will have adequate resources to pay full benefits for the next 26 years".

To be honest, the trust fund is nothing but a collection of IOU's. The money went out the door as soon as it was collected to pay for anything the United States Government needs, including financing a war.

It's been said many times that President George W. Bush "borrowed" $1.37 trillion to pay for his tax cut for the rich and to finance the Iraq war, but we can't prove this since there is no financial transparency from the United States Government.

In a speech at the University of West Virginia at Parkersburg in 2005, then President George W. Bush said "A lot of people in America think there is a trust, that we take your money in payroll taxes and then we hold it for you and then when you retire, we give it back to you.

But that's not the way it works, there is no trust fund, just IOUs that I saw firsthand".

The Social Security Trust Fund has been a "Pay-as-you-go" system for more than 50 years and by law the U.S. Treasury is required to take the surplus and, in exchange, issue interest-accruing bonds to the Social Security Trust Fund (Administration, 1935). Not only President Bush borrowed money from the trust fund, every single president has done it since the fund exists.

I can now see why the Social Security Trust Fund can run out of money, in fact, other countries have followed the same model of "borrowing" from the funds to pay back at a later time, usually 30 to 50 years to let other generation repay what they have spent.

But wait a second, if they continue deporting illegal immigrants, the Social Security Trust Fund will have more money collected than benefits to be paid, and since the Social Security Administration announced that they are increasing the benefit payments by 2% starting on January 2018, the biggest increase since 2012 and to adjust the cost of living, or Cost of Living Adjustment (COLA, that in the Spanish language means TAIL). The average amount a Social Security beneficiary receives is $1,300 a month, so the increase is a big $26 a month, less than a $1 a day.

Please wait! don't spend all the money just now, if the average inflation rate in the United States is 2% as of October 2017 and the Social Security benefits adjustment for 2018 is 2%, your benefit check does not represent an increment because your buying power has been reduced.

The following table shows the funds generated by illegal immigrant deportations since 1993 and kept by the United States Government. The total amount does not represent a liability to the Social Security Trust Fund because those funds WILL NEVER BE PAID.

Source	Funds Generated – 1993-2017
Clinton, Bush, Obama and Trump Administrations from 1993 to 2017	$665,680,467,262
TPS, DACA and DAPA Programs	$61,689,600,000
Temporary Workers Programs	$10,927,872,000
2017 Deportations (Assuming 500 Daily Deportations from October 1st to December 31st, 2017)	$3,965,760,000
TOTAL	$742,263,699,262 *

* This number will be growing every day as deportations are being performed.

Visit www.DeportationsForMoney.com for an up-to-date amount.

Chapter 10: Family Separation

In its greedy desperation, the United States Government is indiscriminately deporting men and women disregarding their family status, the great majority of these individuals are married with U.S. citizen children. These actions are creating family separations and trauma to children that still don't understand the cruelty and brutality of the United States Government. In the near future we will see American citizens with deported parents living in other countries and maybe without an opportunity to reunite them.

However, there is an official immigration form available to re-enter to the United States after an individual has been deported (USCIS, Application for Permission to Reapply for Admission into the United States After Deportation or Removal, 2017). But this form is not a guarantee that someone will be allowed to return to the United States after deportation, especially when that individual represents a liability to the Social Security Trust Fund because he or she has previously contributed to that fund for a great period of time, normally 25 years.

Also, knowing how politicians react at the idea of returning money to you, it would be morally ethical and honest to return all or part of the Social Security money retained by the government, but, I don't expect the United States Government to return any of the money contribution made by illegal immigrants. I am pretty sure that they would prefer to pass a "law" that will confiscate that money, the same way they confiscate assets to drug traffickers.

There are millions of cases of families being separated because one or two persons in that family are being deported. This is systematically done by the United States Government without taking into consideration the anxiety and suffering these poor people go through, for the government they are only numbers and dollar signs.

What is going to happen to their children, mother, father, cousins and their entire community? The United States Government and Congress don't have any kind of feelings for these people, this is inhumane and coldhearted to the extreme specially for the trauma that this action creates on children, who usually are American citizens because they were born in the United States of America, a government that has always promoted protection for the innocent, in this case their own fellow

Americans. Is that because of the color of their skin? Only god knows what they have in their hearts, if they have one.

And how about their homes, mortgages, cars, loans and other personal belongings? The United States Government may confiscate them because money is the only thing important in this case.

More than 95% of the individuals being deported have a full and steady job, have been working for more than 15 years and have never committed any crime, their only crime is to look for a better future for their families, and most important, for having contributed to the Social Security Trust Fund and Medicare for too many years.

But the hate we see in America today has been here long ago since the Europeans came to America in the 1500's to kill Native American Indians and Native Mexicans to steal their land and also because they did not have the color of their skin. Today? No change.

They are indirectly killing all these individuals, either because they are being deported to countries that are crippled by gang violence and drug cartels that do not respect human life. The majority of deported immigrants have never gone back to their home countries in more than 20 or 30 years and have lived in the United States since they were very young.

For the children being technically deported, because they were born in the United States and are American citizens, is a death sentence. They have never been in the country they are being deported to, don't speak the language and don't know their culture. They are an easy target for gangs, drug dealers and criminals. If they don't get killed, they may join these criminals in their activities and may come back to the United States anytime they want, because they are American citizens.

By giving us a "band-aid" solution in the present, the consequences of these actions may create a greater problem in the future. We may be creating hatred in the heart of these children that they may bite our asses in the near future.

History repeats itself, the Spanish-American philosopher George Santayana observed that "Those who don't remember the past are condemned to repeat it", in 1980 the United States saw a threat to the nation and heavily invested in a civil war in El Salvador, thousands of refugees came to the United States fleeing the war, the United States Government granted refugee status to all of them knowing their participation in that cruel war. Later that year a gang known as the MS-13 (Mara Salvatrucha; also known as MS or Mara) was created in Los Angeles, California with members from El Salvador, Honduras and Guatemala.

In the second part of the 80's decade, the majority of this gang (or at least the most dangerous criminals) were being deported back to their home countries. El Salvador was recuperating from a civil war thanks to the United States and the Soviet Union with an exceptional participation of Cuba. Honduras and Guatemala, as neighboring countries, were also being affected by this war.

After creating the war in El Salvador where nobody won, only El Salvador lost and Salvadorians were displaced from their home land, now, the United States Government is filling those countries with the gangs created in the United States and being sent back to their home country.

The gangs are now extorting money from people and killing anyone who refuse to give money to them, at the same time they are recruiting young people by force and killing the ones that are not accepting their terms.

Now entire families along with young people are coming to the United States looking for security and trying to save their lives. They do have a reason to come to America and ask for either political asylum or refugee status and it should be granted to them, this is at least what the United States could do.

Was this mess created by the United States of America? I think it was. The United States Government has a duty to protect all the people that were displaced because of their political ambitions and the control the American Empire wants to have in the world.

There are millions and millions of cases of families being separated, one of them is the case of Jorge Garcia who was brought to the United States when he was 10 years old, now the 39-year-old landscaper from Lincoln Park, Michigan is being deported, his wife Cindy Garcia who is an American citizen and his children a 15-year-old daughter and 12-year-old son also American citizens were crying near the security gates at the Detroit Metropolitan Airport where he was boarding a plane back to his native Mexico.

Garcia lived and worked in the United States for 30 years and never had any problems with the law, his only crime was to be here illegally, but the bigger crime was that he has contributed to the Social Security Trust Fund and Medicare for too long... He had reached the "magic number" and qualify for the "Deportation Proceedings" program.

With almost 25 years of contribution, an equivalent of $110,160.00 in Social Security and Medicare taxes and about $144,000.00 in Federal and State tax contribution, he was in the blacklist of target immigrants to be deported. That's more than a quarter of a million dollars, not too bad for the government because Garcia left the country voluntarily, so the government didn't have to spend a dime.

This is another method ICE officials are using to "brain-wash" future deportees by telling them that if they leave voluntarily, they have a great chance to return to the United States, it is a big lie, they just look for ways to avoid the cost of deportation. In late 2017, ICE officials told Garcia that he could stay with his family for the holidays, but had to leave the country by January 15, 2018.

In the summer of 2017, Liliana Cruz Mendez from El Salvador was deported, she had been living and working in the United States for over 11 years and had reached the "magic number" to qualify for deportation.

Cruz Mendez has two American citizen young children who had to be left in America while she returned to her native El Salvador. Steve Bermudez, her 10-year-old son wrote multiple letters to ICE officials pleading that his mother stay in the country because he and his little sister, a 4-year-old, need her.

One of the letters that Steve wrote said "Plz don't deport my mom", which didn't work because Liliana was deported on June 14, 2017. ICE officials may have responded to Steve with a middle finger.

With a contribution of more than $44,064.00 to the Social Security and Medicare and around $57,600.00 in Federal and State taxes, her time was due.

Deportation is a death sentence for thousands of families, especially children that are the most vulnerable and are the target of criminal gangs, young girls are exploited by prostitution rings and killed if they don't obey the criminals' instructions.

Deportations for Money

By the end of June 2017, more than 22,000 Hondurans were deported back to Honduras, among them more than 2,100 were children. They were sent back to the most dangerous country in the world, Honduras is now known as "the murder capital of the world".

The FOSDEH (Social Forum for External Debt and Honduran Development) published a detailed report (Honduras, 2016) about deported Hondurans and its social and economic consequences.

In conclusion, the United States Government has created the social and economic instability in the Central America region and cannot accept the responsibly or resolve the problem for this messy situation. The chaos in the White House are reflected in poor countries and the people of these countries are suffering the greediness of the American Empire.

The Empire now claims that they are deporting criminals only, they are not deporting American citizen children, they are only deporting their parents and giving the children to relatives. Once the relatives get the children, they bring them to their parents without any expense on the government side, cleaver! That's what I call SOFT-DEPORTATION, which translates in "Deport one, self-deport ten".

I just pray that the American citizen children now being deported don't grow with resentment and hate towards their own country, this could be very dangerous for the United States in one or two decades from now, they can become our worst enemies.

In the 1970's and 1980's, the United States created the Nicaraguan Revolution, the Iranian Revolution, the Contra-Revolution in Nicaragua, the Iran-Contra scandal, the Civil War in El Salvador, the Invasion of Panama and the Invasion of Grenada which displaced millions of families from their own territory.

Now in the 21st Century we have the Invasion of Afghanistan, the Invasion of Iraq, the military Intervention of Libya and the Syrian war that also displaced millions of innocent people in that region.

I am pretty sure that all those events were executed "under the law" and they follow the "law of the land", how about the "laws of laws"?

"For every action there is an equal and opposite reaction".

After all these imperialistic actions, what the United States Government expect? Flowers, gold rain or a loving world? Nice try!

Index

M

magic number, 27
magic numbers, 26, 33
Mara Salvatrucha, 40
Mexico, xi, xii
Modern day slavery, 4

N

November 6, 1986, xi

O

Obama Administration, 15

P

Pay-as-you-go, 36
Policies for the Apprehension,
    Detention and Removal of
    Undocumented Immigrants, xii
President Obama, 35
protect Americans, 12

R

Roman Empire, 6

S

Social Security Trust Fund, xii

T

temporary programs, 27
Temporary Protection Status (TPS), xiii
Thomas Jefferson, 5
too much power, 5
Trinidad and Tobago, xii
Trump Administration, 16

U

United Slaves of America, 3
United States Empire in America, 6

W

white men in Washington, 3

References

Administration, S. S. (1935). *Social Security Act of 1935*. Retrieved from Social Security Act of 1935: https://www.ssa.gov/history/35actii.html

DHS. (2015). *Yearbook of Immigration Statistics 2015*. Retrieved from Yearbook of Immigration Statistics 2015: https://www.dhs.gov/immigration-statistics/yearbook/2015

DHS. (2017, September 5). *Deferred Action for Childhood Arrivals (DACA)*. Retrieved from Deferred Action for Childhood Arrivals (DACA): https://www.ice.gov/daca

DHS Releases End of Year Fiscal Year 2016 Statistics. (2016, December 30). (Department of Homeland Security) Retrieved September 15, 2017, from Official website of the Department of Homeland Security: https://www.dhs.gov/news/2016/12/30/dhs-releases-end-year-fiscal-year-2016-statistics

Estimates of the Unauthorized Immigrant Population Residing in the United States. (2012, January 1). Retrieved from Official website of the Department of Homeland Security: https://www.dhs.gov/immigration-statistics/population-estimates/unauthorized-resident

FAIR. (2017, 10 1). *How Many Illegal Immigranats are in US?* Retrieved from How Many Illegal Immigranats are in US?: https://fairus.org/issue/illegal-immigration/how-many-illegal-immigrants-are-in-us

Fiscal Year 2017 ICE Enforcement and Removal Operations Report. (2017, 12 5). Retrieved from https://www.ice.gov: https://www.ice.gov/removal-statistics/2017

Honduras, D. t. (2016, 12 29). *Deported to Honduras*. Retrieved from Deported to Honduras: http://www.fosdeh.com/wp-content/uploads/2017/02/Deportados-2017-Honduras.pdf

Immigration Reform and Control Act of 1986 (IRCA). (2016, September 9). Retrieved from Official Website of the Department of Homeland Security: https://www.uscis.gov/tools/glossary/immigration-reform-and-control-act-1986-irca

Deportations for Money

Individual Taxpayer Identification Number. (2017, September 9). Retrieved from Internal Revenue Service: https://www.irs.gov/individuals/individual-taxpayer-identification-number

Policies for the Apprehension, Detention and Removal of Undocumented Immigrants. (2014). Retrieved from Policies for the Apprehension, Detention and Removal of Undocumented Immigrants: https://www.dhs.gov/sites/default/files/publications/14_1120_memo_prosecutorial_discretion.pdf

Rasmussen, W. D. (1951, September). *A history of the emergency farm labor supply program, 1943-47.* Retrieved from A history of the emergency farm labor supply program, 1943-47: https://archive.org/details/historyofemergen13rasm

Social Security and Medicare Withholding Rates. (2017, April 14). Retrieved from Internal Revenue Service: https://www.irs.gov/taxtopics/tc751.html

SSA. (2016, 12 31). *Social Security Trust Investments.* Retrieved from Social Security Trust Investments: https://www.ssa.gov/oact/progdata/transactions.html

State, U. D. (2017, 11 15). *Temporary Worker Visas.* Retrieved from Temporary Worker Visas: https://travel.state.gov/content/visas/en/employment/temporary.html

U.N. International Labor Organization. (2016). Retrieved from U.N. International Labor Organization: http://www.un.org/en/sections/nobel-peace-prize/international-labor-organization-ilo/index.html

United Nations Office on Drugs and Crime. (2017). Retrieved from United Nations Office on Drugs and Crime: http://www.unodc.org/gsh/

USCIS. (2011, 9 7). *Temporary (Nonimmigrant) Workers.* Retrieved from Temporary (Nonimmigrant) Workers: https://www.uscis.gov/working-united-states/temporary-nonimmigrant-workers

USCIS. (2017, 11 13). *Application for Permission to Reapply for Admission into the United States After Deportation or Removal.*

Retrieved from Application for Permission to Reapply for Admission into the United States After Deportation or Removal: https://www.uscis.gov/i-212

USCIS. (2017, 11 6). *Temporary Protected Status*. Retrieved from USCIS: https://www.uscis.gov/humanitarian/temporary-protected-status

Yearbook of Immigration Statistics 2015. (2017, May 17). Retrieved from Official website of the Department of Homeland Security: https://www.dhs.gov/immigration-statistics/yearbook/2015

www.ingramcontent.com/pod-product-compliance
Lightning Source LLC
Chambersburg PA
CBHW030030290326
41934CB00005B/562